TIPS FOR PASSING PSYCHOMETRIC TESTS

BULLET GUIDE

Bernice Walmsley

Hodder Education, 338 Euston Road, London NW1 3BH

Hodder Education is an Hachette UK company

First published in UK 2011 by Hodder Education

This edition published 2011

Copyright © 2011 Bernice Walmsley

The moral rights of the author have been asserted

Database right Hodder Education (makers)

Artworks (internal and cover): Peter Lubach

Cover concept design: Two Associates

British Library Cataloguing in Publication Data: a catalogue record for this title is available from the British Library.

10 9 8 7 6 5 4 3 2 1

The publisher has used its best endeavours to ensure that any website addresses referred to in this book are correct and active at the time of going to press. However, the publisher and the author have no responsibility for the websites and can make no guarantee that a site will remain live or that the content will remain relevant, decent or appropriate.

The publisher has made every effort to mark as such all words which it believes to be trademarks. The publisher should also like to make it clear that the presence of a word in the book, whether marked or unmarked, in no way affects its legal status as a trademark.

Every reasonable effort has been made by the publisher to trace the copyright holders of material in this book. Any errors or omissions should be notified in writing to the publisher, who will endeavour to rectify the situation for any reprints and future editions.

Hachette UK's policy is to use papers that are natural, renewable and recyclable products and made from wood grown in sustainable forests. The logging and manufacturing processes are expected to conform to the environmental regulations of the country of origin.

www.hoddereducation.co.uk

Typeset by Stephen Rowling/Springworks

Printed in Spain

To my husband William for his continuing support and patience

About the author

Bernice Walmsley is a specialist writer in business, self-help and education.

After a career in sales and marketing – mainly in the transport industry – spanning 20 years, she became a freelance writer working with local businesses. Her first book, *Succeed at Psychometric Testing – Numerical Reasoning*, was published in 2004.

With an educational background in psychology and politics, she has now had more than 20 books published, including five as a ghostwriter.

Acknowledgements

My thanks must go to the editorial team at Hodder for all their help in producing this book and to Alison Frecknall whose friendly help and guidance were essential to the commissioning process.

Bernice Walmsley
Middlewich, Cheshire
May 2011

Contents

	Introduction	vi
1	Understanding psychometric tests	1
2	Preparation	13
3	Verbal reasoning tests	25
4	Numerical reasoning tests	37
5	Spatial reasoning tests	49
6	General tests	61
7	Other types of test	73
8	Specialized tests	85
9	Yet more practice	97
10	What next?	109
	Further reading	120

Introduction

Many people will have to take part in psychometric tests and most will feel some trepidation at just the thought of them. These tests are held by employers and other organizations, such as universities, that want to **assess the abilities and skills** of applicants and thereby whittle down the numbers to something more manageable.

To help overcome any fear of such tests, this book aims to demystify them and provide information about how to prepare for them. It is this preparation that will help not only to **improve performance in the tests** but also **to increase self-confidence and reduce stress**, and by doing so reduce fear of the tests.

This book aims to demystify psychometric tests and provide information about how to prepare for them

There are many different types of test that can be selected by employers to assess the particular skills and knowledge that they believe are important. These tests fall into six broad categories:

1 **numerical reasoning**
2 **verbal reasoning**
3 **spatial reasoning**
4 **knowledge-based**, e.g. based on mechanical principles
5 **personality tests**
6 **specialized**, e.g. those used by the police or the Armed Forces.

Whatever the tests to be taken, it is important to note that performance in them can be improved by **good preparation**.

The two most important aspects of that preparation are **practice** and **familiarity** with the tests to be taken – and this book will help you with both.

1 Understanding psychometric tests

What are psychometric tests?

Psychometric tests are used to **check the abilities of candidates** by evaluating how they perform specific tasks or react to certain situations.

Aptitudes in a number of areas such as use of numbers or verbal reasoning skills can be tested. The **format will be standardized** and the **results compared with how others have performed**.

Many tests are carried out using a computer but they may also be paper-based.

...knowing how to prepare for psychometric tests is essential...

Understanding a little about the thinking behind psychometric tests will help if you have to sit them and knowing how to prepare for them is essential. So in this chapter we will look at:

* the **types of test** you may encounter and what they are used for
* the **importance of practice** and the sort of practice that will be useful
* tips on how to **prepare** for tests
* **problems and pitfalls** you may encounter.

Who uses them – and who takes them?

The most common use of psychometric testing is by employers trying to **evaluate candidates for jobs**. They will either be administered by the employers themselves or by a specialist company engaged for the purpose.

Psychometric tests are also used in the education sector to select students from applicants seeking places at university.

It follows therefore that a large number of people – just like you – could find themselves sitting one of these tests during the course of their education and/or career.

> **'Always bear in mind that your own resolution to succeed is more important than any one thing.'**
> Abraham Lincoln

Many factors can affect your performance in tests including:

* your **preparation**
* lack of **confidence**
* **stress**
* conditions in the test centre.

You can improve most of these yourself. The main thing is to practise in order that you are prepared. This will give you **more confidence and reduce stress**.

The environment in which you take the tests may be outside your control but if there are any problems you should let the administrator at the centre know at the earliest opportunity.

● Preparation is the key to success.

Different types of test

Many aptitudes can be assessed by psychometric testing as well as your suitability for various careers. Psychometric tests encompass:

* **verbal reasoning** – to test your understanding of written information
* **numerical reasoning** – to see how well you can use numbers
* **abstract reasoning** – to test your reasoning powers using patterns
* **diagrammatic reasoning** – to determine if you can make logical deductions
* **personality tests** – to assess if you are suitable for a particular type of career
* **clerical aptitude** – to test if you can process information accurately
* **mechanical reasoning** – to test your knowledge and understanding of physical and mechanical principles
* **data checking** – to see if you pay accurate attention to detail
* **specialized tests** – to assess your suitability for entry into the Armed Forces, the Civil Service and the police.

Many aptitudes can be assessed by psychometric testing as well as your suitability for various careers

The tests given will vary according to the needs of the organization giving them. An employer may be looking for craft apprentices, for example, and will be keen to see how much you understand about mechanical principles; another employer may wish to check whether your personality type is suitable for a senior management role.

A combination of tests will usually be selected to give **a picture of your capabilities and aptitudes**. It is essential to practise for each type of test and you will have the opportunity to practise several of the different types later in this book.

General tips

There are four important things you should remember when facing a psychometric test of any kind:

1 **Read (or listen to) the instructions carefully** – and follow them precisely. It's easy to fail by ignoring an instruction.
2 **Don't panic** – almost everyone else will be feeling nervous. Furthermore, it is often impossible to complete the tests in the time allowed.
3 **Work quickly** – but as accurately as you can.
4 **Practise, practise, practise**.

By following these simple bits of advice you will improve your score and make taking tests a less stressful experience.

'Success is a science; if you have the conditions, you get the result.'

Oscar Wilde

The most important tip is **to become familiar with the types of test you'll be taking and then to practise. Practice has been proven to improve your score** and will also help you to feel more confident.

If it is some years since you left secondary education, it is likely there will be some gaps in your skills. If you have a mathematics degree, for example, you may not have used much in the way of verbal reasoning skills while you were at university; if your degree is in English, then numerical subjects may be a problem for you.

So, **research the kind of tests you will have to pass** and then **practise as much as you can**. Try to make your practice sessions as close to a real test as possible. For instance, work in a quiet area where you are unlikely to be disturbed.

Problems and pitfalls

All exams and tests have **pitfalls**, so try to avoid them:

* **Make sure you're writing your answers in the right place** – it's easy to misread the answer sheet and get no marks because your answers are in the wrong place.
* **Follow the instructions**.
* **Don't let nerves get the better of you** – most people feel nervous and, of course, a lot will be riding on the test results. But remember that tests are not the only thing you will be judged on – there will usually be an interview and your CV will also represent you.

10

Attention to detail and building your confidence through plenty of practice will help. In addition, **good preparation will always pay dividends.**

During your preparation:

* Get assistance from the people conducting the tests – **sample tests** and some guidelines are usually available. If not, ask.
* **Practise in test conditions.**
* Consider **other types of practice** – word puzzles, number games, etc.
* Try to **stay positive**. This can help to increase confidence and calmness.
* Make sure you're on top form on the day.
* Make sure you know where the test centre is and how long it will take you to get there.

2 Preparation

The importance of practice

It has been proved that **everyone can improve his or her test score** by practising. Unfamiliarity gets in the way of your natural ability, so **practice is an invaluable form of preparation**.

You should aim to become **familiar with the test formats** and **how to tackle the variety of questions** that you may face. Practise for up to two hours per day.

...practice is an invaluable form of preparation

●●

Hopefully you're now convinced about the value of practising and will do plenty of it. In this chapter we look at what else you can do to **prepare yourself for your psychometric tests**. This includes:

* doing **puzzles** to increase your word power
* **using data** to improve your numerical ability
* **relaxation**
* **exercise**
* **preparing** for the day
* having a **strategy** for the test, including careful timing.

Anything that gets your mind working along the same lines as the tests or gets you ready for the day itself will be helpful in the run-up to the tests.

Other types of preparation

Apart from the all-important practice using test examples, there are four main areas of preparation:

1 other sorts of practice, which include:
   a **improving your numerical abilities** by using every opportunity to make mental calculations, examining data such as financial reports and train timetables, or brushing up your basic maths skills with the help of a text book
   b **increasing verbal reasoning** by using word games, crosswords and so on or improving your command of English by studying a book on grammar
2 preparing your **mind and body**
3 setting a **strategy** for the test
4 **practical preparations** for the day.

'Natural abilities are like natural plants; they need pruning by study.'

Sir Francis Bacon

Whenever you have an important interview or a test to take, it can help to **prepare yourself mentally and physically** for the challenge. Worrying about your test results will not improve your performance. If you are really worried about taking the test, the following will **help to reduce stress**:

* listening to relaxation tapes
* meditation
* yoga
* hypnotherapy
* stress counselling
* positive visualization
* an exercise regime.

Your aim should be to arrive at your test in a calm, controlled state of mind.

● **An exercise regime will help to reduce stress.**

Test strategy

Apart from timing (more about this later) there are several ways you can help yourself during the test:

1. If you are really struggling with a particular question, do not waste time. Finding a difficult question can be unnerving but move on – there may be later questions that you find easy.

2. Try not to let people around you affect your performance. Just because the person at the next desk to you has turned over a lot more pages than you, it does not mean that you are doing badly. They might have got all their answers wrong!

3. With numerical tests consider to what degree you should estimate your answers.

Even when you are sitting in the test room, you can still improve your chances of success. Remember:

* listen to – and comply with – the instructions given by the test administrator
* work through the example questions if supplied
* read the instructions on the test paper – they will usually tell you how much time is allowed, whether you may write on the paper (or if rough paper is supplied), whether the use of calculators is permitted, exactly how you should indicate your answers, and how to make alterations if necessary
* work through the questions methodically – and read them carefully.

'Men are born to succeed, not fail.'
Henry David Thoreau

Timing

The time allowed for the various tests will range from just a few minutes to perhaps as much as 40 minutes. If you are being tested on a number of aptitudes, the testing session may well take up to two hours in total.

The important thing is to **use your time wisely**. It is rare that too much time will be allowed for a test; you are more likely to run out of time.

You will therefore need to:

* **Work quickly** while trying to be as **accurate** as possible.
* Try not to let one question take up too much of your time. If a particular question is proving difficult for you, **move on**. You can always come back to it later.
* **Keep going steadily** right through to the end of the test.
* Aim at a balance between **speed and accuracy**.

TOP TIP

It would be unusual for someone to get all the questions right, so it is better to attempt every question and get some wrong than to spend too long on one difficult question.

'**Believe you can and you're halfway there.**'

Theodore Roosevelt

21

On the day

Some **planning** around the practical details will help you to take your test in a **calmer state and give a better performance**. The following may help:

* make sure you know where the test centre is located
* leave for the centre in good time
* get a good night's sleep before the day of the test
* get everything you are taking with you ready the day before
* eat breakfast on the day
* if you have specific requirements – e.g. wheelchair access – let the administrators know in advance
* dress appropriately – if there's an interview, make sure you're smartly dressed.

'Early to bed and early to rise makes a man healthy, wealthy and wise.'

Benjamin Franklin

* When you get your test papers (or start the test on a computer), **make sure you've understood the instructions**. If in doubt, ask.
* Don't waste time reading through the entire test. Start with the first question and **work swiftly and methodically** through the test.
* If you've time at the end, go back to any questions you've missed.
* Before you leave the test centre find out the mechanism for **getting feedback**.
* Celebrate that you have finished!

3 Verbal reasoning tests

What is verbal reasoning?

...your ability to understand, interpret and analyse written information is a skill essential to most jobs

Tests in verbal reasoning assess your ability to understand, interpret and analyse written information and it is, of course, a skill essential to most jobs.

Usually the questions will take the form of **a passage of text followed by statements about it** that you are required to decide are **'true'** or **'false'** – or, in some cases, conclude there is **'insufficient information to say'** – using only the details given. The passage will often be of a complex nature requiring careful attention.

In this chapter there will be practice questions, together with a section of **tips to help you tackle verbal reasoning tests**. This will be followed by a selection of **test questions along with the answers and explanations**.

Even if you get the test questions correct, it can help to read all the explanations as you may pick up specific tips and the explanations may point out things of which you would otherwise have been unaware.

Tips for verbal reasoning tests

> **'We are what we repeatedly do.**
> **Excellence then, is not**
> **an act, but a habit.'**
>
> Aristotle

It is most important that you fully understand what the possible answers mean:

* **true** – a logical answer given the information in the passage
* **false** – this statement cannot be true given the information in the passage
* **cannot say** – there is insufficient information given to enable you to say one way or the other.

If you understand exactly what you are being asked to do, you are more likely to be able to tackle the questions **with confidence**.

Any reading that helps your understanding of complex information will add to your skills.

You must **only use the information that is given in the passage**. Do not be tempted to bring in any prior knowledge you may have on the topic – this will almost invariably lead you to give an incorrect answer.

Tackle the questions as follows:

* **read** through the passage
* then try the first question – make sure you **understand** exactly what is being said
* locate the **relevant** information and read it again
* **decide** upon your answer.

You are aiming at a balance of speed and comprehension rather than memorizing the passage or guessing the answers.

Try these questions...

To complete these questions, take all the details
describing the incidents, plus the additional
information, as facts. You must then decide about
the truth – or otherwise – of the numbered
statements that follow. Answer:

❋ 'A' if the statement in the question is **true**
❋ 'B' if the statement in the question is **false**
❋ 'C' if it is **impossible** to say whether the
   statement is **true or false**.

Allow yourself 25 minutes.

At 8.30 a.m. two children were hurt when a car hit them on a zebra crossing on their way to school. The car did not stop. Later a red car was found abandoned. We also know that:

* nobody saw the accident but a red car was reported being driven recklessly nearby at 8.35 a.m.
* at 6 a.m. the owner of the red car reported it stolen from his drive
* the children were not accompanied by an adult.

Now decide whether these statements are 'true':

Q1   The driver should have stopped after the accident   [   ]

Q2   The red car injured the children   [   ]

Q3   The red car was stolen   [   ]

Q4   The two children attended the same school   [   ]

More practice questions

Several thefts from garden sheds were reported in Midhampton during August but the police have no leads as to who is responsible. In September in nearby Oxdown, Peter Cornwell reported the theft of a lawnmower. We also know that:

* Peter had two lawnmowers
* several youths had been trespassing in gardens in Midhampton
* the police do not believe the incidents in Midhampton and Oxdown are connected.

Now decide whether these statements are 'true':

Q5 Recently recovered goods can now be returned to their owners [ ]

Q6 Several expensive items of equipment were stolen from the sheds [ ]

Q7 The youths broke into the sheds [ ]

Q8 The thefts from the sheds occurred in August [ ]

A six-week-old baby girl was found dead by her mother when she went to collect her from her cot on Friday 4 September. The woman's elder daughter called an ambulance and the police. We also know that:

* a neighbour reported that the baby was often left alone in the house
* the local social services had visited the family twice prior to the baby's death
* the police told the mother that the death was being treated as suspicious.

Now decide whether these statements are 'true':

Q9 The baby was the woman's only child [ ]

Q10 This was a 'cot death' [ ]

Q11 The neighbour had called the local social services [ ]

Q12 The mother killed the baby [ ]

Answers and explanations

Q1 A – it is true the driver (whoever he was) did not stop but certainly should have

Q2 C – there is no real evidence here to link the red car with the accident

Q3 A – the car was reported stolen earlier that morning

Q4 C – the two children *may* have attended the same school but it is not possible to say for sure

Q5 C – we do not know whether or not any goods have been recovered

Q6 C – we do not know whether or not the items stolen were expensive

Q7 C – although the youths were trespassing, there is no evidence to link them to the thefts

Q8 C – the thefts were reported in August but they could have occurred earlier

34

Q9 B – we know that the woman had two daughters as her elder daughter raised the alarm

Q10 C – this is an assumption and will be one of the things considered by the police

Q11 C – it could be true that the neighbour had called the local social services but we do not know for sure

Q12 C – the mother will be under suspicion but we are not given any information that proves her guilt

Remember, it is vital you only use the information given and do not make assumptions or use any other knowledge you may have.

4 Numerical reasoning tests

What is numerical reasoning?

Numbers are everywhere – so understanding them is vital

• •

Numerical reasoning tests **check your ability to understand, and work with, numbers**. Numbers are everywhere – so understanding them is vital to your everyday performance.

Many employers want to check the ability of potential recruits to **add, subtract, divide and multiply**, and extract information from **tables, graphs and charts**.

All these skills will have been learned at school and practice will help us to remember them.

Being adept with numbers is an **essential skill** – don't assume you can always use a calculator. Just consider the different things – both at home and work – for which you need to use your numerical skills:

* shopping bills
* volume discounts
* money-off promotions
* tables (such as train timetables)
* budgets and targets
* VAT calculations.

In this chapter, we'll look at a few tips on taking tests involving numbers and then try some practice questions.

Tips for numerical reasoning tests
...taking every opportunity to practise using numbers will ensure better results

It has been proved that **anyone can improve their score** in this type of test by practising, so anyone doubting their numerical abilities should practise. Becoming **familiar** with the types of questions and taking every opportunity to practise using numbers will ensure **better results**. Speed and accuracy will improve with practice, not only with test questions but also with numbers used in daily life.

Opportunities to practise in everyday life include:

* adding up shopping bills
* reading financial information in newspapers
* planning a rail journey using train timetables
* calculating VAT
* working out deals and promotions
* checking your pay slip
* comparing currency exchange rates.

Now some tips about working with numbers:

* work out **figures in brackets** first
* with graphs and charts, **take note of details** around the diagram
* **negative numbers** multiplied by negative numbers always give positive answers
* treat multiple-choice answers as suggestions – it may be possible to **estimate**
* make sure you're **writing your answer in the right place** – it's easy to lose track if the answer sheet is separate.

Try these questions...

Answer the following general mathematical questions
without using a calculator:

Q1 $(99 \div 11) - 4 = $ ____?   **Q5** $(28 \times 3) \div 3 = $ ____?

Q2 $(1{,}933 + 11) \div 3 = $ ____?   **Q6** $\frac{1}{4} + \frac{1}{2} + \frac{1}{4} = $ ____?

Q3 $4 - 5 - 7 + 33 = $ ____?   **Q7** One third of 99 $= $ ____?

Q4 $150 \times 6 = $ ____?

42

CASE STUDY: Practice adds up to new job

John left school at 16 and had always struggled with numbers.
When he knew he had to pass a numerical reasoning test for a job,
he started to practise by checking his bills, pay slips, etc. He gained
confidence, improved his mental arithmetic and got the job!

Bullet Guide: Tips For Passing Psychometric Tests

Use a calculator for these questions:

Q8 5% of 25,500 = ____ ?

Q9 Workers are paid £8.00/hour. If each of five staff worked 42 hours per week, what was the total paid per week?

    a) £1,500 b) £168 c) £1,680 d) £336

Q10 What is 49% of £15?

    a) £7.35 b) £5.00 c) £6.75 d) £5.75 e) £6.25

Q11 1.5 × 45 = ____ ?

Q12 0.33 + 1.5 + 25 = ____ ?

Find the **missing number** in these sequences:

Q13 70, 80, 160, 170, 340, ____ ?

Q14 4, 12, 36, 108, ____ ?, 972

> **TOP TIP**
> Become familiar with using your calculator before you take a test.

More practice questions

Use the pie chart to answer the following questions:

Q15 How many people entered the examination?

Q16 Approximately what percentage of entrants formed the largest score group?
a) 10% b) 25% c) 50% d) 90%

Q17 If the pass mark was 51, how many people passed?

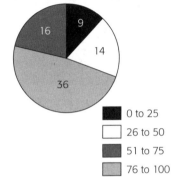

Figure 4.1: Examination marks

0 to 25
26 to 50
51 to 75
76 to 100

Q18 How many people were in the two highest-scoring groups?

Q19 How many more people obtained scores of 51% or over than obtained scores of 50% or less?

Q20 If the pass mark was 51, how many people failed?

Use the table to answer the following:

Table 4.1: Exhibition attendance figures

Category	Number of exhibitors	Number of visitors
Catering companies	25	188
Packaging suppliers	6	62
Distributors	7	29
'Cash and carry'	9	45

Q21 What was the total number of visitors?

Q22 Which category of exhibitor had the second-highest number of visitors?

Q23 Which two categories had a total of 13 exhibitors?

Q24 What was the average number of visitors per 'cash and carry' exhibitor?

Q25 How many visitors did the categories of distributors and 'cash and carry' have in total?

Answers and explanations

Q1 5 – do the calculation in brackets first

Q2 648

Q3 25 – don't let the negatives throw you

Q4 900

Q5 28 – did you spot that the division and the multiplication cancel each other out?

Q6 1 – a simple fraction

Q7 33 – divide by three to get a third

Q8 1,275 – calculating 5% is easy: it's half of 10%

Q9 c) 1,680 – try estimating this one

Q10 a) £7.35 – 49% is nearly 50%, which is the same as a half, i.e. £7.50

Q11 67.5 – one and a half times 45

Q12 26.83 – simple addition, but watch the decimal point

Q13 350 – here you need to spot a pattern: add 10, double it, add 10 and so on

Q14 324 – three times the previous number

Q15 75 – add together all the groups

Q16 c) 50% – did you see this from your last answer?

Q17 52 – add together the two groups

Q18 52 – a different way of asking the same question as the last one

Q19 29 – work out the two totals (over 51% and under 50%) and take one from the other

Q20 23 – add the two lowest-scoring groups

Q21 324

Q22 Packaging suppliers

Q23 Packaging suppliers and distributors

Q24 5 – divide 45 by 9

Q25 74

How did you do? Don't worry if you got one or two wrong – practice makes perfect!

5 Spatial reasoning tests

What is spatial reasoning?

Spatial reasoning tests look at the **relationship between a series of shapes** and will help an employer to assess your **problem-solving abilities**.

There are a number of different types of spatial reasoning tests, which may also be called:

* **inductive** reasoning
* **abstract** reasoning
* **diagrammatic** reasoning.

All will use shapes and diagrams to assess your abilities.

It is believed that spatial reasoning tests can indicate intelligence without penalizing candidates on grounds of culture, language or reading ability.

Finding relationships between figures can be an easy task – if you know what you're looking for. So in this chapter we'll look at a few tips, then provide some practice questions – with answers and explanations as before – to give you a better understanding of how to tackle tests that assess your problem-solving abilities in this way.

Spatial reasoning tests can indicate intelligence without penalizing candidates on grounds of culture, language or reading ability

Tips for spatial reasoning tests

These tests require you to **work with shapes in a number of ways**.

Sometimes you will be given a set of shapes or figures and you're then required to work out which of a number of other figures also belongs in the first set. The idea is that you will **perceive the relationship** between the figures in the first set and then pick out the one in the second set that will **fit that relationship**.

Or you may have to visualize the shapes in a different way – **fitted together or rotated**, for example.

Working with shapes is something that you can practise in everyday life.

Spatial/abstract reasoning tests are similar to verbal and numerical reasoning tests – they use **shapes, diagrams or symbols, rather than words or numbers**, to test your ability to spot relationships.

To succeed at this sort of test, you will need to seek out **opportunities to practise**. Try:

* solving jigsaw puzzles
* drawing diagrams
* taking note of symbols used in everyday life – road signs, notices, etc.
* cutting out shapes and arranging them to form different shapes
* drawing patterns
* doodling using geometric shapes
* rotating solid shapes – cans, bricks, etc.
* visualizing shapes
* imagine how a room you're familiar with would look from another angle – say from the ceiling, looking down.

In short, try to see all the shapes and symbols in the world around you.

Try these questions...

Each of the shapes will have at least one side labelled with a letter. You must decide what these shapes will look like **when they are put together with the sides marked with the same letters next to each other**.

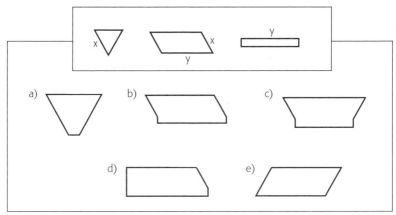

Figure 5.1: Q1

Bullet Guide: Tips For Passing Psychometric Tests

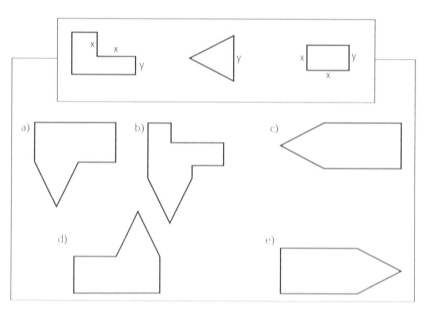

Figure 5.2: Q2

More practice questions

In these questions you are shown two three-dimensional objects, each with a dot placed in one corner. You must decide, from the choices given, which option **shows the same objects rotated and with the dot placed in the correct corner.**

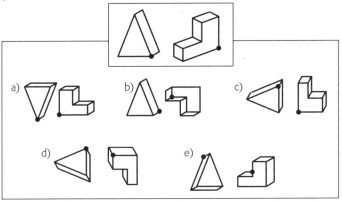

Figure 5.3: Q3

Figure 5.4: Q4

Answers and advice

In the first two questions you must match up the letters that are marked on the shapes. The shapes that are the answers to the questions are 'exploded' for you in Figures 5.5 and 5.6, allowing you to see how the three shapes in each question have come together – with the x and y sides matching – to make the new shape.

Figure 5.5: Answer to Q1: c)

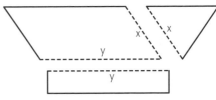

Figure 5.6: Answer to Q2: e)

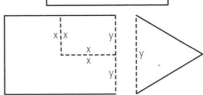

For the second set of questions – which use three-dimensional objects and require you to visualize what they will look like when they have been rotated – **note the answers then look back at the objects** in the tests so that you can work out how they have been rotated. Pay particular attention to the dots placed on the objects. It may help you if you note a particular feature of each drawing – e.g. a right angle – and then work out where the dot is in relation to this.

Answer to Q3: c)

Answer to Q4: e)

> ## 'An ounce of practice is worth more than tons of preaching.'
>
> Mohandas Gandhi

6 General tests

Tackling different tests

There is an enormous variety of tests that an employer or organization can choose

Many people fear – or at least are slightly nervous about – taking psychometric tests. Mostly this is a fear of failure or a fear of the unknown. **Familiarity**, and **practice wherever possible**, can help to overcome this fear.

Finding out what tests are being set is vital. There is an enormous variety of tests that an employer or organization can choose and enquiring about the test process will always help.

In this chapter there will be examples of a few different tests that many people have difficulty with or would like to know more about. Some you can practise for (e.g. tests involving fractions) and some you cannot (e.g. personality tests). It's always best to know what you're facing, so we will take a look at:

* **personality** tests
* tests involving **percentages, fractions and decimals**
* **algebra** tests – e.g. Civil Service quantitative relations tests
* **reasoning**.

This chapter will also provide the answers to the different tests and advice on tackling some of the questions.

What are personality tests?

Many employers and other organizations believe that **certain personality types are more suited to specific jobs** and will conduct personality tests accordingly. For example, they might want someone who will have the ability to lead a team or someone who is a creative thinker and problem solver and will rule out anyone who does not possess these personality traits.

Personality tests aim to assess those **aspects of a person's character that do not change throughout their lifetime**. Most people would agree that it is not possible to improve your performance in these tests. So, are you an introvert or an extrovert? A leader or a follower? An optimist or a pessimist?

Although you cannot prepare for personality tests, a quick look at the sorts of questions you may be asked may **help to allay any fears**. Typical questions may include:

* do you prefer to leave a party early or stay to the end?
* do you prefer working in a team or alone?
* do you dislike being late?

Note!
Questions in personality tests will be asked in different ways to stop 'second-guessing'.

● Employers want to know if you have the right personality traits to climb the career ladder.

Percentages, fractions and decimals

Although percentages, fractions and decimals may seem varied, the way in which the calculations work is very similar. **Percentages are closely related to fractions** in that percentages are expressed in parts of one hundred, e.g. 50% is 50 parts of one hundred and could also be expressed as 50/100ths or ½, i.e. one half.

Decimals are also closely connected – the decimal point separates the whole number from the decimal fraction. You may also encounter ratio calculations in this section.

Try these questions:

Q1 45% of £15 =

a) £7.75 b) £5.00 c) £6.75 d) £5.75 e) £6.25

Q2 $9\frac{5}{8} - 6\frac{1}{4} =$

a) $4\frac{1}{2}$ b) $3\frac{3}{8}$ c) 2 d) $3\frac{1}{4}$ e) $3\frac{5}{8}$

Q3 5.35 + 14.9 − 2.33 =

    a) 22.58 b) 21 c) 18.0 d) 17.92 e) 18.82

Answers and explanations

Q1 c) £6.75. Remember that 45% is the same as 45/100ths. You could divide £15.00 by 100 then multiply by 45, or you could work out 45% of £10 and then multiply by 1.5 – whichever you find easiest.

Q2 b) 3⅝. You need to find the common denominator. In this case it is 8, as both 8 and 4 – the two denominators – will go into this. It is then relatively easy to answer, i.e. 9⅛ − 6⅞ = 3⅝.

Q3 d) 17.92. Make sure you get the decimal point in the right place – by keeping everything lined up.

Algebra tests

These tests are also known as **quantitative relations** tests and are useful practice for the UK Civil Service Fast Stream Qualifying Tests. They test your ability to use algebra to solve numerical problems.

Your task is to identify the numerical relationship in the first four rows and then to apply that same relationship to the final row to find the missing number.

Use algebraic formulae to find the missing figure (?) in the final row:

Q1	A	B	C
	3	2	5
	5	4	7
	9	5	17
	12	11	14
	12	?	10

Q2	A	B	C
	4	6	6
	7	2	19
	9	6	21
	5	1	14
	10	?	27

Answers and explanations

Q1 13 – the formula is: $3A - 2B = C$
so $(3 \times 12) - (2 \times ?) = 10$
therefore $? = 13$

Q2 3 – the formula is: $3A - C = B$. If you multiply the value of A (10) by 3 and subtract the value of C (27), you will arrive at the value of B (3).

If you have difficulty with algebra, this simple explanation may help:

$A + 8 = 10$

Now, just one glance will tell you that A must equal 2 but how did we solve this formula? The method is firstly to isolate the item that we are trying to find by removing the 8 from the left-hand side. To keep the balance we must also remove the 8 from the right-hand side:

$A + 8 - 8 = 10 - 8$

and this is equivalent to: $A = 2$

Reasoning tests

This sort of test will assess your **ability to understand words**. You will need to select the correct word from the choices given:

Q1 Sweet is to sugar as sour is to:

   a) banana b) vinegar c) potato d) bread e) food

Q2 Chapter is to book as verse is to:

   a) poem b) rhyme c) writing d) poet e) newspaper

Q3 Wheel is to car as rudder is to:

   a) sailor b) ship c) steer d) train e) sail

Q4 Dark is to night as light is to:

   a) midnight b) day c) sunshine d) bulb e) noon

Q5 A lot is to many as hardly any is to:

   a) countless b) numerous c) few d) inadequate e) least

Answers

Q1 b) vinegar

Q2 a) poem

Q3 b) ship

Q4 b) day

Q5 c) few

In this sort of test you need to make **logical connections between the words**. To take the last question as an example, look at the two words given in the question – what is the connection? 'A lot' means almost the same as 'many', so you must then look in the list of suggested answers to find a word that means something similar to 'hardly any'.

In this sort of test you need to make logical connections between the words

7 Other types of test

Preparing for sets of tests

...employers are looking for people to do jobs that demand specific skills

There are lots of different types of test – some will test for different **knowledge** (e.g. technical aptitude) and some will test your **range of skills** (e.g. data checking).

All will be set by employers who are looking for people to do jobs that demand specific skills. These will usually form a battery of tests and, of course, it is always useful to **practise for them appropriately**.

This chapter looks at general tests that employers may include in a test battery in addition to the more common verbal and numerical reasoning tests.

Sometimes it helps to study the knowledge required, as it will to become familiar with the different types of test you may face. These tests will cover:

* **technical aptitude**
* **clerical aptitude**
* **mechanical comprehension**
* **data checking**.

Technical aptitude tests

These tests will usually be given to people applying for **jobs with a craft or engineering element**. They may encompass different sorts of knowledge and skills:

* **physical** principles
* **mechanical** principles
* **fault-finding** skills
* **analytical** skills.

It's important to remember that employers are looking for people suited to technical work. If that's you, it is likely that you already possess the knowledge and skills. You could study some aspects of this knowledge, but if it doesn't interest you sufficiently or you don't have the skills, then there would be little point in getting such a job.

'There's place and means for every man alive.'

William Shakespeare

Try these questions:

Q1 Which of these helps to keep a car stable?
   a) low centre of gravity b) a narrow wheelbase c) a high centre of gravity d) high speed e) low speed

Q2 What is the opposite of acceleration?
   a) speed b) deceleration c) movement d) force e) ascension

Q3 What unit is used to measure force?
   a) ohm b) ampere c) Newton d) volt e) tension

Q4 What does perpendicular mean?
   a) deep b) weak c) unstable d) at right angles e) high

Q5 How many mirrors do you need to make a periscope?
   a) 4 b) 3 c) 1 d) 2 e) none

Answers

Q1 a); Q2 b); Q3 c); Q4 d); Q5 d)

Clerical aptitude tests

Employers recruiting to **clerical positions** will often use the following tests:

* ❋ **work rate**
* ❋ **verbal reasoning** – see previous tests
* ❋ **numerical ability** – see previous tests
* ❋ **data checking** – covered later in this chapter
* ❋ **typing**
* ❋ **computer use**.

These are all elements of clerical work and the number and type of tests given will depend on the specific role. In using these tests an employer will be aiming to employ people with an **attention to detail** and thereby avoid costly errors that could be made by clerical employees. They will select candidates who pass the test and show they have the aptitudes that have been identified as essential.

'Ambition should be made of sterner stuff.'
William Shakespeare

Try this brief extract from a work rate test:

Q1 Which could be an alternative code for PQR?

P	Q	R	M
4	8	5	2
•	V	◆	☐

a) M☐5
b) 4V5
c) PV•
d) 2◆8
e) ◆52

Q2 Which could be an alternative code for 297?

T	L	E	I
9	7	4	2
◆	•	☐	V

a) T◆2
b) IE☐
c) VT•
d) L•☐
e) ET•

Answers

Q1 b); Q2 c)

Work rate tests are aimed at ensuring you can work **accurately at speed** so there will **not usually be sufficient time** to complete them.

Mechanical comprehension tests

These tests assess your **understanding of mechanical principles and your ability to work with mechanical concepts** and are frequently used by organizations that are looking for people to **fill technical roles**. They will usually involve knowledge of pulleys, electrical circuits, levers and gears, and an interest in this sort of subject helps here.

If you have the knowledge in this area, you will choose the correct answer. But if you have difficulty, a good book on the subject will help.

Now try these questions:

Q1 How many millimetres in a metre?

   a) 10 b) 100 c) 1,000 d) 10,000 e) 100,000

Q2 Why is steel a common building material?

   a) it is bendy b) it is strong c) it can be painted any colour
   d) it is light e) it is heavy

80

Q3 Through what can heat NOT be transferred by convection?

a) liquids b) solids c) air d) steam e) gases

Q4 What changes the amount that a bicycle moves forward with each pedal stroke?

a) electric power b) pedals c) wheels d) gears e) wind

Answers

Q1 c) 1,000

Q2 b) it is strong

Q3 b) solids

Q4 d) gears

Data checking tests

These tests are often given to applicants for **clerical or administrative** jobs and will consist of 20 or more questions. They assess **how quickly and accurately you can detect errors in data**, which has obvious advantages for jobs where attention to detail is important.

The data to check could be a series of numbers (account numbers, for instance) or words (a list of addresses, for instance) or a combination of the two.

82

Here are some **tips for success**:

* **check each character individually** rather than simply reading
* there may be more than one error in each piece of data
* try to **maintain concentration** throughout the test.

Compare the two lists and mark the differences in the right-hand list:

Answers

| Q1 | 8555948 | 855948 | Q1 | 8555948 |

Q1 8555948   855948   Q1 8555948

Q2 6722343   6722334   Q2 6722334

Q3 1006008   1006008   Q3 No difference

Q4 6 Newton Street   6 Newton Road   Q4 6 Newton *Road*
    Provdale   Promdale   Pro*m*dale

Q5 Mr B Williams   Mr B Williams   Q5 Mr B Williams
    144 High St   144 High St   144 High St
    Colchester   Colchaster   Colch*a*ster

Q6 B Dyer   B Dyer   Q6 B Dyer
    97 Meadow View   87 Meadow Views   *8*7 Meadow View*s*
    Northtown   Northtown   Northtown
    OL3 5NN   OL3 3NN   OL3 *3*NN

8 Specialized tests

About specialized tests

...organizations design their tests to assess the skills they need in recruits

Specialized tests are those set by organizations that **have particular requirements and will test applicants accordingly**. Organizations such as the Armed Forces and the Civil Service have identified **specific skills and aptitudes** that they require in their employees.

Practising with many of the general tests in this book will help with the specialized tests but specific materials for each are available from the websites of the relevant organizations.

The tests discussed in this chapter are those set by:

* the British Army
* the Royal Navy
* the Royal Air Force
* police forces
* the Civil Service
* universities.

Because of their particular recruitment requirements, these organizations design their tests to assess the skills they need in recruits. Knowing what they are looking for is the first step to being prepared and this chapter will give brief details to guide you.

The Armed Forces

Each of the British Armed Forces has its own battery of tests for applicants, designed to ensure they get the sort of entrants they require. Here is a summary of the tests for each organization:

British Army

* **Reasoning** – problem-solving questions
* **Letter checking** – carrying out a checking process
* **Number distance** – calculate the differences between three numbers
* **Odd one out** – select from a group of three words
* **Symbol rotation** – spatial awareness

Royal Navy

* **Reasoning** – process information
* **Verbal ability** – relationships between words
* **Numeracy** – working with numbers
* **Mechanical comprehension** – basic mechanical concepts

Royal Air Force

* **Verbal reasoning** – using written information
* **Numerical reasoning** – arithmetic, tables, graphs, etc.
* **Work rate** – coding exercises
* **Spatial reasoning** – working with shapes
* **Electrical comprehension** – basic electrical concepts
* **Mechanical comprehension** – working with mechanical concepts
* **Memory** – remembering information

In addition to the psychometric tests for each of the forces, you will have to pass medical and physical examinations, attend interviews and fulfil specific conditions of employment. Details are available on their websites:

89

* www.army.mod.uk
* www.royalnavy.mod.uk
* www.raf.mod.uk.

'Belief creates the actual fact.'

William James

Police recruitment tests

The assessment to enter a police force in the UK is divided into five distinct parts:

1 **numerical reasoning** – your ability to use numbers
2 **verbal logical reasoning** – drawing conclusions from descriptions of situations that a police officer may meet
3 **competency-based structured interview** – how you have dealt with specific situations in the past
4 **written exercises** – producing a letter and a report about a specific situation
5 **interactive exercises** – acting as a customer services officer.

These are all standardized tests carefully designed to assess your suitability for the role of police officer.

During the tests and exercises you will be observed and your performance assessed against pre-set criteria based on the **seven core competencies**:

1   respect for race and diversity
2   teamworking
3   community and customer focus
4   effective communication
5   problem solving
6   personal responsibility
7   resilience.

These core competencies are the background to all the tests – it is vital you understand what they mean.

In addition to the competency tests, you will also have to pass a medical examination and a physical fitness test. Once you have been accepted, there will be a two-year probationary period including foundation training before you qualify as a police officer.

The Civil Service

The tests you will have to pass to enter the UK Civil Service will depend on the level at which you want to enter and the type of work you want to do. The pathways available are the **Fast Stream** management programme for graduates, clerical entry and separate programmes for certain government departments. There are **five different options** in the Fast Stream recruitment:

1 Analytical
2 Human Resources
3 Technology in Business
4 European
5 Northern Ireland.

Options are selected during the application process.

Note!
Entry into the Civil Service is subject to nationality requirements in addition to passing the psychometric tests.

The Fast Stream entry involves a number of steps:

1 **online self-assessment** – verbal and numerical reasoning tests to see for yourself if you want to take it further
2 **online practice tests** – optional but recommended
3 **online selection tests** – verbal and numerical reasoning tests plus a competency questionnaire.

Good results in these first steps will lead to further progression:

4 selection of career **options**
5 **e-application** form
6 **e-tray exercise** – at a regional centre
7 **assessment centre** – in London.

This is obviously a lengthy process and will involve lots of effort and some travel but this is the **starting point for a career in the Civil Service**.

University admission

Some universities will require you to pass an **admissions test** in addition to gaining a specific number and grade of A-levels. These tests form part of, among others, applications to study **medicine, dentistry or law** at many universities and a number of subjects at Oxford and Cambridge.

These tests include:

* BioMedical Admissions Test (BMAT)
* English Literature Admissions Test (ELAT)
* Sixth Term Examination Paper (STEP)
* Thinking Skills Assessment (TSA).

These tests assist the universities in differentiating between equally qualified candidates and are designed to ensure equal opportunities. They are often administered in schools and colleges and at a variety of test centres.

94

The Cambridge Thinking Skills Assessment, for example, consists of 50 multiple-choice questions to test your **critical thinking and problem-solving skills**. Ninety minutes are allowed for its completion.

Typically, questions will ask you to spot flaws in arguments or define the main argument in a short passage. You may also be asked to solve diagrammatic problems where your spatial reasoning skills will be tested.

The best way to prepare for tests of this kind is to follow recommendations issued by the institute to which you are applying, which are usually available on their website or by post. As for other types of test, the best preparation is gaining familiarity with the tests to be taken and practising wherever possible.

Typically, questions will ask you to spot flaws in arguments or define the main argument in a short passage

9 Yet more practice

Mixed tests

...the value of practice in improving your chances of success

Hopefully you will now have recognized the value of practice in improving your chances of success.

As you have seen there are a great many types of test that you may be set. Your **first task** will be to find out just what tests you will be sitting and then do some practice. In addition to the tests featured in this book, you could also **search out** other ways to practise.

In this chapter you can try a variety of questions from different test types, which will help you to pinpoint any potential problems you may have while gaining more practice.

Questions are included from some of the most common sorts of test, such as numerical ones involving word problems or graphs and charts as well as different sorts of verbal reasoning ones.

The answers are given at the end of this chapter.

'**Always desire to learn something useful.**'
Sophocles

Try these questions...

Answer the following questions without using a calculator:

Q1 $1,934 + 24,555 - 18 = ?$

Q2 $(16 \times 3) \div 8 = ?$

Q3 $-12 + 8 = ?$

You may use a calculator to answer these questions:

Q4 $3/4 + 2/3 = ?$

Q5 $2\frac{1}{4} \div 3 = ?$

Q6 $1/2 \div 4 = ?$

Q7 If every 250 bottles of bleach require 16.25 litres of solvent to produce, how much solvent is required to produce 6,500 bottles of bleach?

a) 42.3 litres b) 100.0 litres c) 121.9 litres d) 422.5 litres

Q8 Last year's sales target was £265,000. This year's is £328,000. By what percentage has this year's sales target increased over last year?

a) 17% b) 29% c) 43% d) 81% e) none of these

100

Use Figure 9.1 to answer
the next three questions:

Q9 If labour costs
were excluded,
what would be the
production costs per
100 of Product A?

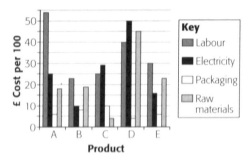

Figure 9.1: Production costs

a) £103 b) £101
c) £49 d) £51 e) £25

Q10 What is the total cost per 100 of the most expensive product to
produce?

a) £119 b) £54 c) £139 d) £172 e) £103

Q11 Which is the least expensive product to produce?

a) product A b) product B c) product C d) product D e) product E

More practice questions

A reasoning test now – **read and memorize the sentence given, then answer the question relating to it**:

Note!
In actual tests you will not see the question on the screen at the same time as the answers.

Q12 Pete is taller than Sam. Who is shorter?
  a) Pete b) Sam

Q13 Norman arrived earlier than John. Who arrived last?
  a) Norman b) John

Q14 Pam has lighter hair than Sue. Who has darker hair?
  a) Pam b) Sue

Q15 David reads fewer books than Andrew. Who reads more books?
  a) David b) Andrew

Q16 Carole has more shoes than Barbara. Who has fewer shoes?
  a) Carole b) Barbara

Let's try another test involving words. Each question consists of three words. Two of the words will be connected – they may be opposites or have similar meanings. Your task is to spot the connections and **find the odd one out**:

Q17 a) fat b) bus c) thin

Q18 a) common b) rug c) carpet

Q19 a) sail b) also c) boat

Q20 a) bad b) good c) drastic

Q21 a) seven b) zoo c) animal

...and yet more practice questions

Now for some numerical problems – this time using words. **Try these without a calculator**:

Q22 Five friends go to a restaurant and spend £127.50. If they share the bill equally, how much would they each have to pay?

a) £30.00 b) £25.50 c) £25.00 d) £51.00 e) £127.50

Q23 If your taxi fare comes to £17.50 and you add a 10% tip, how much would you pay in total?

a) £19.25 b) £22.00 c) £17.50 d) £15.75 e) £19.50

Q24 A printer produces eight pages per minute. How long – in hours and minutes – would ten copies of a document consisting of 64 pages take to print?

a) 10 hours 40 minutes b) 3 hours 10 minutes c) 1 hour 20 minutes d) 1 hour 30 minutes e) 76 minutes

And a few **number sequence questions** to finish:

Q25 29, 30, 32, 35, 39, ?
    a) 41 b) 42 c) 46 d) 45
    e) 44

Q26 45, 67, 89, 101, 112, ?
    a) 63 b) 131 c) 123 d) 132
    e) 109

Q27 155, 165, 170, 180, 185, ?
    a) 195 b) 200 c) 190 d) 205
    e) 210

Q28 70, 80, 160, 170, 340, ?
    a) 350 b) 360 c) 370 d) 380
    e) 400

Q29 512, 256, 128, 64, 32, ?
    a) 30 b) 20 c) 16 d) 8 e) 4

Q30 81, 87, 84, 90, 87, ?
    a) 90 b) 93 c) 96 d) 84 e) 81

Q31 1, 3, 3, 9, 27, ?
    a) 48 b) 36 c) 243 d) 241
    e) 263

Q32 2, −4, 6, −8, 10, ?
    a) −14 b) 14 c) −10
    d) −12 e) 12

Q33 16, 17, 19, 22, 26, ?
    a) 27 b) 28 c) 29 d) 30
    e) 31

Q34 1, 8, 27, 64, 125, ?
    a) 244 b) 216 c) 198 d) 224
    e) 220

Answers and advice

Q1 26,471

Q2 6 – always work out the calculation in brackets first

Q3 −4 – remember that negative numbers are still numbers

Q4 1⁵/₁₂ – finding the common denominator of 12 makes this one easy

Q5 ³/₄ – try converting the fraction to ⁹/₄

Q6 ¹/₈ – to divide by four, multiply the denominator by four

Q7 d) 422.5 litres – 6,500 divided by 250, multiplied by 16.25

Q8 e) none of these – try estimating this one (none of the answers are near the approximate 25% increase)

Q9 c) 49 – add the three remaining cost areas for this product

Q10 c) £139 – concentrate on the two possibles: products A and D

Q11 b) product B – work out the total production costs for each product

With these questions, it can help to rephrase the question:

Q12 b) Sam **Q13** b) John **Q14** b) Sue **Q15** b) Andrew **Q16** b) Barbara

For these questions, find the two words that are related – they may be opposites or similar. These are the odd ones out:

Q17 b) bus **Q18** a) common **Q19** b) also **Q20** c) drastic **Q21** a) seven

Work systematically with numerical word problems:

Q22 b) £25.50 **Q23** a) £19.25 **Q24** c) 1 hour 20 minutes

With number sequences, you're looking for the relationship between the numbers:

Q25 e) 44	**Q29** c) 16	**Q33** e) 31
Q26 b) 131	**Q30** b) 93	**Q34** b) 216
Q27 a) 195	**Q31** c) 243	
Q28 a) 350	**Q32** d) – 12	

10 What next?

What to do after the test

The important thing is not to give up but to continue with the job search

• •

The period immediately after taking a test can be an uncertain and worrying time. The important thing is not to give up but to continue with the job search. This can take the form of obtaining feedback, researching other job opportunities or assessing – and perhaps revising – plans for your next career move. Remember – your life is your responsibility.

'It is thrifty to prepare today for the wants of tomorrow.'

Proverb

In this chapter we will look at what you can do after you have completed a test. This will cover:

* how the tests are **scored**
* getting **feedback**
* finding out more
* **career planning** – your next steps
* **assessment centres**.

It's important not to think the job is done once you have taken the test. **Everyone must take responsibility for their own job search and take action** – whatever the results of the tests taken.

How tests are marked

There is no way for you to know, before you start, how the test will be scored. Some tests award points for completing more questions, some deduct points for incorrect answers.

However, your score will be **standardized** to those of other candidates in your peer group – don't forget, **you are competing with others**. Scores are usually calculated using a **percentile scoring system**. Therefore, even if you know how many answers you got right, this does not translate into a percentage score but into a percentile rating relative to a known distribution.

Whatever your result, remember that tests are only **part of the selection process** and it is possible to **improve with practice**.

'Self-confidence is the first requisite to great undertakings.'

Samuel Johnson

When you do these tests you are being **assessed for your suitability for a job**, according to what the prospective employer has decided are the skills and aptitudes required. Therefore your results should not be viewed as 'pass' or 'fail' – instead view the tests as an exercise **exploring where you would be best suited**. There is little point in getting the wrong job so do not allow the results to dent your self-confidence.

Obtaining feedback

Many test administrators will have **procedures in place to give feedback** or it may be up to you to **ask for it**. When you get it, consider:

* If you've been successful – celebrate! And then prepare for the next step.
* If you've not passed, **don't take it personally**.
* You may not agree with the results – but that does not necessarily make them wrong.
* Ask questions – **where do you need to do better?**
* How can you **improve your performance** next time?
* Get **advice** about your options.

At this stage – whether you've passed or failed – you will need to assess your results and work towards your future.

If, after very careful consideration, you think the result may be wrong, you will need to **proceed with caution**. You could:

* ask to sit the test again – especially if you can show you were not well or were disadvantaged in some way on the day of the test
* make a complaint – but you must be sure of your facts
* move on.

Most results are found to be correct and will inevitably reflect the requirements of the organization carrying out the tests. It may be best to simply resolve to prepare better next time.

'Luck is what happens when preparation meets opportunity.'

Seneca

Planning your future

If your tests have gone well, you may be on the way to the career of your dreams. However, what can you do if you've not been successful? You have three choices:

1 **ignore it and carry on** – this may not get you anywhere
2 **improve your performance** – more practice could get you a good result in the future
3 **review your career plans**.

Much will depend on your personality, abilities and aspirations. At this stage you may find yourself having to look carefully at your future. How you proceed will determine the outcome so it is essential to plan carefully.

'Need teaches a plan.'

Irish proverb

How you react to your test results will depend on:

* **Your choice of career** – If it's very specific, such as joining a police force, then your only choice might be to look for something different. But if you're trying for a general position, you may wish to keep trying different organizations.
* **Your results** – If your tests, for example, show some improvement in numerical ability will get you where you want to go, then more practice will help.

Some planning for the future will never be wasted and you should review your abilities and requirements and set out a **personal development plan** for the next few months.

Planning for the future will never be wasted and you should review your abilities and requirements and set out a personal development plan

About assessment centres

In essence, assessment centres are **extended selection procedures** and being invited to one takes you a step closer to getting a job. They usually consist of a **series of tests and interviews** conducted over a day or more and are designed to reduce the number of applicants. Many employers use them, including:

* **large multinationals** looking for graduate trainees
* **public sector** organizations, e.g. the police or Civil Service
* large **financial institutions**
* **management consultancies**.

Assessment centres provide employers with lots of information and can be prepared for in the same ways as any tests. The only difference is they may take longer and be more concentrated.

The kind of tests you could face include:

* **psychometric tests** – as you will know by now, these test your numerical, verbal and spatial reasoning skills
* **group exercises** – these test your ability to work in a group, possibly in a discussion on a set topic or a task, e.g. a puzzle
* **in-tray exercises** – you are given a work situation and, using the information, you must make decisions
* **presentations** – this may be a short talk you must give to the other candidates or to the selectors
* **social interaction** – although this may not be a formal test, you will be observed meeting, eating with and possibly socializing with other candidates
* **interviews** – these may be more in-depth than previous ones.

Further reading

Kourdi, Jeremy, *Succeed at Psychometric Testing: Practice Tests for Verbal Reasoning Advanced* (Hodder Education, 2008)

Rhodes, Peter, *Succeed at Psychometric Testing: Practice Tests for Critical Verbal Reasoning* (Hodder Education, 2006)

Rhodes, Peter, *Succeed at Psychometric Testing: Practice Tests for Diagrammatic and Abstract Reasoning* (Hodder Education, 2008)

Vanson, Sally, *Succeed at Psychometric Testing: Practice Tests for Data Interpretation* (Hodder Education, 2008)

Walmsley, Bernice, *Succeed at Psychometric Testing: Practice Tests for Numerical Reasoning Advanced* (Hodder Education, 2008)

Walmsley, Bernice, *Succeed at Psychometric Testing: Practice Tests for the National Police Selection Process* (Hodder Education, 2008)